CELESTIAL JOYRIDE

Books by Michael Waters

Celestial Joyride 2016
Selected Poems (UK) 2011
Gospel Night 2011
Darling Vulgarity 2006
Parthenopi: New and Selected Poems 2001
Green Ash, Red Maple, Black Gum 1997
Bountiful 1992
The Burden Lifters 1989
Anniversary of the Air 1985
Not Just Any Death 1979
Fish Light 1975

Editor:

Contemporary American Poetry (with A. Poulin, Jr.) Eighth Edition, 2006;
　　Seventh Edition, 2001
Perfect in Their Art: Poems on Boxing from Homer to Ali (with Robert
　　Hedin) 2003
A. Poulin, Jr. Selected Poems 2001
Dissolve to Island: On the Poetry of John Logan 1984

CELESTIAL JOYRIDE

POEMS BY
MICHAEL WATERS

AMERICAN POETS CONTINUUM SERIES, NO. 154

BOA EDITIONS, LTD. ❋ ROCHESTER, NY ❋ 2016

First Edition
16 17 18 19   7 6 5 4 3 2 1

For information about permission to reuse any material from this book please contact
The Permissions Company at www.permissionscompany.com or e-mail permdude@
eclipse.net.

Publications by BOA Editions, Ltd.—a not-for-profit corporation
under section 501 (c) (3) of the United States Internal Revenue
Code—are made possible with funds from a variety of sources,
including public funds from the Literature Program of the National
Endowment for the Arts; the New York State Council on the Arts, a
state agency; and the County of Monroe, NY. Private funding sources
include the Lannan Foundation for support of the Lannan Transla-
tions Selection Series; the Max and Marian Farash Charitable Foun-
dation; the Mary S. Mulligan Charitable Trust; the Rochester Area
Community Foundation; the Steeple-Jack Fund; the Ames-Amzalak Memorial Trust in
memory of Henry Ames, Semon Amzalak, and Dan Amzalak; and contributions from many
individuals nationwide. See Colophon on page 88 for special individual acknowledgments.

ART WORKS.
arts.gov

State of the Arts

NYSCA

Cover Design: Daphne Morrissey
Cover Art: "Bateau" by Carlo (1916–1974)
Interior Design and Composition: Richard Foerster
Manufacturing: Versa Press, Inc.
BOA Logo: Mirko

Library of Congress Cataloging-in-Publication Data

Names: Waters, Michael, 1949–
Title: Celestial joyride : poems / by Michael Waters.
Description: First edition. | Rochester, NY : BOA Editions Ltd., 2016. |
    Series: American Poets Continuum Series ; 154
Identifiers: LCCN 2015043379 | ISBN 9781942683063 (paperback)
Subjects: | BISAC: POETRY / Inspirational & Religious. | POETRY / American /
    General. | RELIGION / Philosophy.
Classification: LCC PS3573.A818 A6 2016 | DDC 811/.54—dc23 LC record
available at http://lccn.loc.gov/2015043379

BOA Editions, Ltd.
250 North Goodman Street, Suite 306
Rochester, NY 14607
www.boaeditions.org
A. Poulin, Jr., Founder (1938–1996)

CONTENTS

for Fabian Mircea Waters

What a beautiful word 'Waters' is!
—Emily Dickinson

You are beautiful and you are alone
—Nico

CELESTIAL JOYRIDE

MADRIGAL

—the origin of the word is uncertain, probably from
the Latin *matricalis*, literally "of the womb"

Eyelash, tongue tip, finger whorl.
Scrotum. A skull
Shifting from archipelago to minor
Continent.
       Buoyant contentment.
How I wish I could remember
Such leisurely becoming, that
Slow sprawl toward finale,
And recognize once more,
Before death, the barely
Audible madrigal,
That almost visceral,
Unself-conscious whistling
That summoned me,
Little god roaming twilight,
Farther away from the celestial
Hour by hour—
Earlobe, freckle, sphincter—
So I might mouth its maker.

EFFATA

—the word Christ spoke to the blind man,
Stroking both eyes with spit-damp clay,
His voice imperative, never to be
Disobeyed...
              the beggar birth-blind,

Left to marvel at leaf-light, pollen,
Rainfall, the blunt bodies of birds,
And that first face, the face
Of the One who unveiled his eyes,

Jesu and His command
              Look! Behold! Discern!
On endless loop inside his brain, the man
Afraid to shut his eyes, to sleep, even
To blink for fear of the loss of Heaven,

Christ gone, and no one near or far
To horror miracle into his ear.

BEAUTY IN THE WORLD

So much beauty in the world… trills Macy Gray
And the studio crew claps rhythmically
Into the mic
          clap clap clap clap clap clap clap
As though the response to beauty should be applause,
As in fact it was each summer evening in the '80s
At the outdoor café on the cliff on Ios
Where the rousing final movement of Dvořák
Was synced to the sun's declension
So that the orchestra crescendoed
Then abruptly ceased at the precise moment
The amaranthine disc of sun
Dissolved into the Aegean,
All of us burnt and stoned and giddy
As we burst into applause
Before nimbling the goat paths to hostels
Where we showered in anticipation
Of the modest debaucheries of night.
But it's the applause that stays with me
Rather than the ravers on holiday
In their sheer linens and seamless tans,
The applause and the beauty
That provoked it, the sunset
So elemental in that sparse landscape, the inexhaustible
Swyving of sun and sea, the hissing
We thought we heard below the cellos
And violas and tympani
Less the devil's beckoning tongue
Than the sizzle of skin, perversely
Pleasurable, more than enough
Sacrifice for our sins as we stared all day
At each other's bodies then entered them

Each night, that sibilant *pssst* louder
As flesh touched flesh in imitation
Of sun and sea, in homage to sun and sea,
To so much beauty in the world, O
Macy Gray, I'm clapping along right now
Stopped at the traffic light
Years and miles away from the island
Which still blazes in beauty without me,
Even at this hour when all the young fuckers
Who have followed my hoofprints
Sigh in their sleep
And the sun slips out of the sea
With no one watching, not one
Lost sylph searching for her sandal
Or ghost of shepherd
Or farmer on donkey to begin this day
With the joyful prayer of applause.

PUNK PRAYER

monastery, Eibingen, 12th C
Cathedral of Christ the Savior, Moscow, 21st C

In language of her own wild invention,
Nun & mystic Hildegard von Bingen
Offered prayers only God could ascertain,

Though she must have wondered, slipping again
Into ecstatic visionary daze,
How such odd words resounded in His brain.

Centuries later, God remembers her
As the guitar thrash of Pussy Riot
Explodes in sacrificial orgasm,

The frescoed cherubim & stone-eyed saints
Startled by eccentricity & rage:
Three pierced daughters, each gorgeous in His gaze.

AMERICAN SONGBOOK

The red-tailed hawk twigged together its nest
On a ledge overlooking Central Park
Where in first-light April hours it savaged
Juvenile squirrels and blind, star-nosed moles,
And one dusk swooped to talon a pigeon
Scrounging among jouncy, bug-eyed dealers
Who flashed tin-foiled wares in Washington Square.
Binocular'd birders thrilled to each kill.
Soon city papers reported raptors
Everywhere—you had only to glance up
To find bandages of sky slashed with wings
Or shut away subway rumble to hear
Hatchlings shrill like toy factory whistles.
Some neighbors preferred the more common birds,
Mourning doves, vesper sparrows, thrushes, wrens,
And began to feed these communal choirs.
Susannah McCorkle spotted the hawk
Gliding past the river's indifference
Through the window of her 16th floor flat
As she rehearsed lush, romantic ballads—
As Time Goes By   *My Funny Valentine*
Autumn in New York   *Come Rain or Come Shine.*
The songs soothed her throat like whiskey and smoke,
But also burned, their lyrics so deeply
Incised in her body that a single,
Fevered word—*stardust*—probed some childhood wound.
She undid herself standard by standard.
They Can't Take That Away From Me, she sang,
Until rain remembered to draw a breath;
She crooned *Someone to Watch Over Me*. . . .
One sparrow worrying the hawk's shadow

Circled tarred rooftops on West 86th.
When Susannah McCorkle leapt away
From dawn's unshakeable melancholy,
The sudden displacement of sodden air
Huffed each feather; that bird hesitated,
Then ruptured the upswell for the final   .
Fistful of seed still heaped upon her sill.

d. May 19, 2001

DOMINOES

We set them up to flip them down, made them
   Fall with a flapping sound—whirr of an ace
      Slapped by circling spokes as the boy biked by,
         Or the wound-up skirr of the hummingbird
      Jazzing like fire above honeysuckle.
  It's the long labor for such brief reward
That puzzles, though we arranged the thousand
   Black caskets heliocentrically
      Until forefinger and thumb, pincer-like,
         Locked up, mini-muscles cramped in a row,
      Domino domino domino, so
  Begged to be crooked, dumb flexing Arnolds. *Clack*.
I knelt with my father to watch death flow.

POEM, SLOW TO COME, ON THE DEATH OF LOGAN

1923–1987

1: 1970: Brockport, New York

You perched on the edge of my roommate's
Vacant bed
Like some featherless, ungainly bird
Ready to swoop down upon
Roadside carrion,
Then plunged below
The narrow
Comfort of my quilt
To clasp me within your burdensome
Yearning.
       Naked,
You wrapped loose flesh around me
Like a ragged cloak, enfolding
Chest and waist and thighs, blunt beak
Seeking out my cock
Till I squirreled free, dressed in darkness, then fled.
In the student lounge I found my roommate
Dozing among night owls. "You too?" he said.

John, you came on to all the worshipful
Boys, then mothered them, prodded
Poems, instilled some semblance of voice.
We came to be friends, even though
I was your second choice.

2: 1987: San Francisco

From higher ground you plunged once more,
One final swoop
From the ledge of your Post Street roof.
No one knows if you leapt or were flung
By some rough trade thug
You'd hoped to seduce
Rather than pay. You had no money anyway.
Scabbed, alcoholic, cruising slanted streets,
You ignored your friends'
Stabs at salvation: food, camaraderie, that warmth
You craved but could not find.

John, no one I've ever known
Was as ravenous
For the solace flesh can give,
For the poetry that welled up within you,
That poetry (and flesh) by which you lived,
Its blood overflowing, like hurricane waters,
Your cast-off body's blurred borders.

3: 1971: Brockport, New York

Hung over, we three gathered
One fall morning at the Church Street diner.
Desperate to be one of you, *très* cool,
I preened and lied, "And when I awoke,
I could not remember her name!"
"Oh," shrugged Al, "I'm so beyond that.
I wake up and wonder, Is it a man or is it a woman?"
"Oh," you intoned, nailing me in my place,
"I'm *way* beyond that. I open my eyes and pray,
God, let it be human!"

4: 1987: San Francisco

Hospitalized again, you telephoned
The month before you died. I stood shaken
In the kitchen as your remote, tremulous
Voice unspooled the air,
Frightening me. I could hear
Its unbearable fragility.
I recalled the night I first heard you
Recite your poems: sober,
You slurred the words, allowing them
To clamor one within the other,
Drawing out each line's
Voluptuous texture,
Its lush, fleshy, coloratura design.

5: 2012

I still have the note you left in my room
Where you found yourself once again alone,
A penciled scribble on a torn
Corner of notebook paper
Slipped under a plastic cup,
Its final drop
Of watery whiskey gone:
Dear Mike and other party-goers:
Who
        will forgive me?
Cheers.   *John.*

MARVEL

Consider Bacchus straddling the razor
   Between sensual pleasure and formal
Debauchery. *Psilax. Mainomenos.*
   The boy who looped cold links around his neck,
Zapped on doggie tranqs and José C,
   Rocked that kiddie swing Silver Surfer-style
Through the stars' labyrinthine circuitry,
   Wound that chain like old school industrial
Bling till his eyes tracked streaking satellites,
   Then stepped, doomed hero, onto celestial
Swells, sank into exile and elegy.

Matthew F.
1986–2007

OLD SCHOOL

Seth wrestled the Camaro with one fist & popped
Handfuls of pills while the pistol rode my thigh.
I shouted *Is it loaded?* over Grandmaster Flash.
Amateur thug, he slipped the piece into his boot
& swaggered like a bouncer into the funeral home.

Sunglass'd still & jittery, he scanned the room,
Swept past uncles to the open coffin, knelt there,
Then wedged the gun between our father's thumbs,
Insurance for the celestial joyride, & tattooed,
Pierced, & fucked up, bowed his shaven skull & wept.

OLD COUNTRY RECIPES

The alley is littered with cabbage leaves
Overflowing the bin of the Jade Garden
Next door to the Ridgewood Funeral Home.
Food and death remain longstanding companions:

Witness the maize preserved with the skulls
Of the few Navajo allowed old age,
Or onyx bowls of peacock eggs
In tombs of the adolescent pharaohs.

After the viewing, immigrant neighbors
Bear consolations of casseroles—
Dim cousins feast, then calm hands urge
Those closest to the deceased

To swallow marrow broth, spoonfuls of noodles,
As if death drills a fathomless well
Only the right measure of soup
And homemade challah might fill.

POTTERY SALE

To raise fare, the amateur potter
Has choreographed her creations—

Birdbath basins like baptismal fonts
Aswirl upon the studio floor, a miniature

Universe starred with secular bowls
Mimicking pineapple halves or split gourds.

We step among the wobbly mugs, each pitched
Forward, handles looped crookedly,

Lips loose, Dali-like, glaze chipped—
Our friend's illness given shape—

This pilgrimage of half-pint penitents
Shuffling off toward Lourdes.

BLACKBIRDS

—found

—as told to Ian Clayton

Do you know, Ian, I'm sometimes working in my back yard
And I can hear my dad whistling.
He's been dead for more than twenty years.

When I look I see a blackbird.

That bird's ancestors must have heard my dad's whistling
And mimicked him. My dad's whistling
Has passed through a lot of eggs to get to that bird I hear now.

TIC TAC TOE

My son's Xs resemble swastikas
In his Tic Tac Toe boxes. Only four,

He's unaware of any history
Other than his own, disinterested

In a universe that doesn't hold him
At its vaginal and radiant core.

I let him win once more, my wobbly Os
Each a contracting galaxy, ready

To be rid of me. Futureless father . . .
While a fathergone future gyres his way.

卐 卐 卐   † † †   XXX   O
No symbol he pencils can make me stay.

SIXTIES SONNET

I have become handsome in my old age.

"You're cute," smiled Denise, breaking up with me,
"But cute is all you'll ever be."

Denise who was so wrongwrongwrong, I miss
Our Woodstock nights, half-a-million thumb-flicked

Bics coaxed to climax by God's thwapping bass,
Hissing soppy Oms against the cloudmass.

A drenched, naked hillside soulless and pure,
Zonked, mud-caked, Yanomamö, immature.

I forgive Sly and the Family Stone.
I slept through Santana, dreaming future

Exes who might love me despite my rage.
I have grown lonesome in my afflictions.

I have become handsome in my old age.

OLD RECORDS

Black as licorice, their lacquer
Dulled by dust & crevassed with scratch,
The stacked records skyline thrift shop bins.

Unsleeved, each displays its long-defunct
Label, its colorful, name-scrawled, inner wheel—
Betty inked on Big Top, *Scotty* looped on Sun—

As each hole awaits its spindle to flaunt
The 45's wavy warp around the turntable.
The stylus clasps the groove, then settles

Into static like the music that must fill
The lightless spaces between stars,
Till the opening notes, slightly bent

But familiar, spiral outward from speakers
To spark the air, to make us sway
As if on shag. Each oldie returns us

To our first love of a word
Synced to a struck snare or an upright
Piano's shattered glass or a single chord

Slashed on a cheap electric guitar,
That word never before so exact, so clear—
Until the now-fuzzy tip of the needle

Stutters in a scratch & one syllable
Insists itself over & over as you stand there
Transported, alive, fifteen once more, 1965.

THE CAPTAIN'S TOWER

I first heard the name Ezra Pound on Saturday, August 28, 1965, yawped by Bob Dylan in a new song, "Desolation Row," performed that night at Forest Hills Tennis Stadium in Queens, New York. I was fifteen.

> And Ezra Pound and T. S. Eliot
> Fighting in the captain's tower
> While calypso singers laugh at them
> And fishermen hold flowers
> Between the windows of the sea
> Where lovely mermaids flow
> And nobody has to think too much
> About Desolation Row

I had no idea that those three syllables formed a name. As they came near the beginning of the line, the syllables sounded more like "*every pound*"—"every pound of T. S. Eliot." Such misheard lyrics constitute a *mondegreen*, the word coined by Sylvia Wright in an essay published in *Harper's Magazine* in 1954 and named after Lady Mondegreen. There was no Lady Mondegreen. The lines of an anonymous 17th-century ballad, "They hae slain the Earl of Murray, / And laid him on the green," are misheard as "They hae slain the Earl of Murray and Lady Mondegreen." Popular song lyrics are rife with such misheard phrasings ("Hold me close and tie me down, sir"), but this time the fault was my own.

The album on which "Desolation Row" appeared, *Highway 61 Revisited*, would be released two days later, so during that week I spun the disc again and again and heard the name repeated until finally it came clear. It was obvious that Dylan had read "The Love Song of J. Alfred Prufrock":

I have heard the mermaids singing, each to each.
I do not think that they will sing to me.
I have seen them riding seaward on the waves.

I had been reading Eliot. But Ezra Pound?

The following Saturday, on the final weekend of summer before high school resumed, I took the F train into lower Manhattan and walked off Sixth Avenue to the 8th Street Bookshop, "the very hearthside of hip, the cynosure of cool," *The New York Times* would claim three decades later. "[T]he person riffling through a book in the next aisle could be W. H. Auden . . . Marianne Moore . . . or perhaps Allen Ginsberg." The poetry books lined the upstairs wall to the right of the staircase, and you could cradle an armful to the front of that second floor where the literary journals wobbled in stacks and where one or two shabby easy chairs had been placed before the window above 8th Street: *the captain's tower.* That's where I slouched that afternoon with several books by Ezra Pound.

What did I read that day—"The River-Merchant's Wife: A Letter"? "In a Station of the Metro," its fourteen words leaping from ghostly human faces to "Petals on a wet, black bough"? "Hugh Selwyn Mauberley" with its "sudden shifts of perspective," its "presentation of an individual consciousness against a panorama of the age," as Richard Ellmann describes the poem? Didn't that also describe what Dylan was doing in "Desolation Row"? Pound was still alive in 1965. He suddenly seemed, as I sat in the 8th Street Bookshop, as vital a presence as The Beatles, as Dylan. "Ezra Pound," I mouthed to myself. Pop music was moving beyond me, and I had to be smarter to catch up.

THE BEATLES

Didn't I laugh with unabashed glee
When I read Aram Saroyan's *The Beatles* (Barn Dream Press, 1970):
"John Lennon
         Paul McCartney
                  George Harrison
                          Ringo Starr"
The entire book! Each name given its separate page
As though their names conveyed
All that could be said about them, and more.
Unacknowledged, I wandered the Strand Bookstore
On the corner of Broadway and 12th
Where in his photography studio in 1887
George C. Cox illuminated "one of the roughs, a cosmos," Walt Whitman,
Whose name five years before his death
Was not yet resonant with myth,
Though he'd once posed with a fake butterfly
Propped on his finger like a wedding ring.
How could we each be solitary, yet
Collectively the same? How could one "contain multitudes"?
John   *Paul*   *George*
                    and Michael

Grown dizzy now
Before miles of books upon miles of shelves,
Wondering how to begin
To inhabit the vast privacies of his name.

THE BOOK OF NAMES

in memory of Adrienne Rich
& for my mother

Dead lovers of our fathers   possessors
Of the once common but then abandoned
Names—
       Edith   Gladys   Theodora   Pearl
Khaki-wackies   leotarded hipsters—
Names given over to modest markers
Thousands of stone loaves splintering sunlight
Their chiseled dates spanning a century
Influenza   polio   HIV
Lynchings   World Wars   the sputtering progress
Of democracy—
            your true names waver
Like heat thumbing asphalt   like history

The lives of others . . .
           Eunice   Clara   Mae
Who charged with rage these out-of-fashion names
Your Dawns and Chelseas candle in sleek throats
To mouth and summon if ever they pray
Prudence   Vera   Faith
           and you:
               Dorothy

EVE'S DAUGHTER

Spring: your mother ammonias soiled windows,
Each chamois gesture returning to glass
A certain beauty always there, but less
Obvious before this moment, the light

After seven days' rain casting judgment

Upon all things with odd clarity: dust
Flared to meaning, your body enraptured
By the hour's whispered solicitations.
Your flown soul unveiled will never be missed:

The glass so clean it no longer exists.

MIHAELA BAREFOOT

When shame wouldn't allow me to look any longer
Into the negative space
Gathering its rough, cotton twill around your temples,

I glanced down to be startled
By the sensual, brush-stroked slashes of your toenails—
Still redder than any girl's.

RADU LUPU

Kennedy Center
Washington, D.C.

"Tell your wife not to wear a short skirt,"
Laughs the ticket broker over the phone,
Weirdly prescient, since he doesn't know my wife
Who enjoys sporting brief, flouncy skirts
That flatter her slender legs. "We've had complaints."
He's convinced me to purchase Chorister seats
For the recital by Radu Lupu, Romanian pianist,
Famous for his interpretations of Brahms
Under the batons of Paavo Järvi and Edo de Waart,
Each of whom he chooses, at times, to ignore,
And for his quick-to-flame all-consuming temper.
Chorister seats are cheap, behind the stage,
Overlooking the piano, so we'll be able to follow
Lupu's muscular fingers as they fondle
Brahms' "Sonata No. 3 in F Minor,"
Admire their reserved and eloquent articulations.
But no late seating, nothing to distract
Concert-goers staring directly at you
From the airy architecture of the concerto.
Lupu lives inside his name, maintaining
That feral, raised-by-wolves demeanor,
Having, like my wife, endured the cruel
Deprivations of post-war communism.
You can see he'd rather be at home
In ragged tee and oversized boxers
Stroking the ivories in an ill-lit room
Than here in the Concert Hall in his tux.
He exhausts himself with formal restraint,
Each note weighted with urgency and grace,
Rhapsody raining onto creation,

All the newly breathing creatures gazing up
From their communal pools of icy rills.
Time commences its swirling, tidal pull.
When the final drop dissolves, rapt devotees
Applaud lustfully as Lupu bows, shakes
The conductor's hand, the concertmaster's,
Then, remembering, turns to face us,
Still clapping in the cheap seats.
He squints—then nods—when he spots my wife.
Here in America, in the pretense of democracy,
No one tells a woman how to dress.

THE SCAVENGERS

—found

Of compost and insects, art may be born.
Some artists scavenge the life sciences
For materials that might surrender
Cosmic verities.
    Fabian Peña
Whose preferred medium is cockroach
("material I can easily find")
Puts their parts to work in his art—
Legs glued into long, lacy cylinders;
Fanned wings, incandescent, subtly rufous,
Configured to render shadow and light.
Christy Rupp constructs model skeletons
Of the dodo, great auk, and other birds
Which humans have driven to extinction—
Life-sized, built with discarded chicken bones
From fast-food restaurants like KFC.
NY artist Tracy Heneberger
Created a 'kind of' samurai shield
Of 1,155 sardines
In a series of concentric circles
Glossy with hyaline coats of shellac.
It was a challenge, the artist stated,
Finding sardines of the right length and width,
Sardines that still had eyes in their sockets,
Sardines lacking the curvature of death.

THE LITTORAL

Las Terrenas
Dominican Republic

Hard to tell if dog or log lies ahead.
Each stick a snake. Each stranger familiar.
The mind labors in mysterious ways,
When it labors at all. Each leaf a leaf.

Often words begin with a walk, although
Silence, like rain, always approaches.
My six-year-old jabbers against silence.
Is that a log or a dog? he worries.

The poem doesn't know yet. *Guess*, it insists.
Meaning to animate the universe,
Dog, I wager (I always wager *dog*),
And on three wobbly legs the wet log lifts.

HORSE

Not ghost horse, fever-dream horse, horse inked on silken fog
Setting off once more the neighbor's neurotic bulldog,

Nor the wan roan of the brief, elliptical lyric
Looping infinities in our pre-dawn cul-de-sac,

But mudwall of muscle in the bicycle's headlamp
And that sulfurous stench stuttered from the twitching rump . . .

The queer horse looms unbridled amid scarred sycamore.
Straddle her:
        let thighs clench ribs. Or
                girdle only air.

DOG EARS

One tattered copy of Rumi's ghazals
With umpteen page corners triangled down:

How a book sleeps on a used bookshop shelf
Until I stroke its spine, slide it away

From twelve R-shelved sisters to swing it home,
First stopping at Discount Liquors, Food Town,

Fruit & Nut Hut, cramming the canvas tote.
Who could dream so busy an afterlife?

Later I scold the previous reader—
Not that poem . . . this one! as I fold over,

Thumb to forefinger, another fig-smeared,
Almond-scented, newly belovèd leaf.

QUOTING RUMI

!My cock's delight and bafflement
Rumi swooned over the Belovèd,
Though Coleman Barks
Never translated *that* poem,
So the lie/line remains my own,
And if in my home
The Belovèd does not assume
One of the unutterable
Names of G-d,
A definition of Whom
In a personal *Devil's Dictionary*
Might read "denial of responsibility,"
Then the Belovèd must be you!
In the '60s flick *Change of Habit*,
The incognito novitiate,
On the verge of final vows,
Finds herself suddenly besotted,
So must choose between
The hunky, guitar-strumming,
Inner-city doctor
And her spiritual vocation.
Elvis . . . or God? Tough one.
Among the thrumming icons
In this world and the next,
I have chosen you, for whom
My cock is a candle illuminating
The gold-spun tapestries of Heaven!—
Lines *probably* spouted by Rumi
Who jotted right-to-left,
Though in a language only a few
Anglo-Americans can decipher.

for Mihaela

JADE GARDEN

To be a man means constant revision
Like correcting a writing, my fortune

Cookie reveals once the moo goo gai pan
Lies razed to rice clumps and water chestnuts.

I read the sequence of lucky numbers—
      2 9 14 34 49
Powerball ticket, you must change my life!

Cool zeros congeal in sesame oil.
Chopsticks sift ciphers in leftover rice.

"We cultivate remorse," smirked Baudelaire,
"As beggars entertain and nurse their lice."

MORNING RUN

Alligator Snapping Turtle
Macrochelys temminckii

for _____

For three days I'd admired them as I looped
The lake, envied their insatiable lust,
The urge primeval that held them coupled
Without regard for noon blare or shadow—

    Triple-ridged & immobile, two turtles
    Clumped in a knoll of biological
    Imperatives, bound in root-rot & branch,
    Charred humps of stone at the sod's algal edge—

Then understood a convergence of boughs
Locked them together, their hinged ritual
Undone nights ago. Nature diminished.
I sneakered, soles mud-sucked, behind beaked jaws

    To clench the rim of horned shell & swivel
    Male from mounted female till both broke free
    & oared for silty depths beyond ruined oaks.
    Two torn creatures. Our mute complicity.

EROTIC AMPHORA

Akrotiri

The passage of time bore no consequence
Undersea.
        Algae measured our patience.
Drowsy since the ash-heaped catastrophe,

We'd stopped counting
              flashing coins of fish eyes.
Hauled by hemp toward sky, our skins sloughed off
Their furzy, vegetal shine.

            We tumesced.
Jealous progeny aahed as once we had,
Swept our flesh awake
          till the lovemaking

We'd desired was granted by laughing gods.
And we shattered
       into one thousand
            shards.

THE NEW GODS

Bulbs ablaze, composed in the bare window,
  Our mirror at this hour, I undress you,
    Nothing but the planetarium's dome

And late winter stars assembling beyond,
  No earthly voyeur to peep inside, though
    Our fantasy flourishes otherwise.

Later, spent in darkness, we memorize
  Snowfall, diminishing rooftops, sclera
    Of streetlamps in parallel rows, autos

Sashaying single-file between auras,
  While the galaxy's imaginary
    Gawkers cluster in the vast milky waste

Of their own making, icy cumulus,
  Attendant still upon our nakedness—
    Gods from whom we chastely avert our gaze.

LAST DAY ON IOS

Blunt nubbins birthed on dainties
Whiffled into your drawer,

The mice pulsated pinkly,
Transparent, six erasers

Lacking graphite to lend them
Purpose, so I swaddled them

In the silk sling of one thong,
Black eye-beads absorbing

The wince-sharp blast of sky
Out of which wings gyred

As I fluttered the tribe onto stubble,
Six micey nougats, six snouty baubles,

Babes whisked by beaks
To raucous treetop nurseries.

For how many hours did my shadow
Needle our garden, startled

By first knowledge of our fate?—
To be driven naked and ashamed,

Imparadised
Beyond the unlatched gate.

SICK STUDENT

"I look around me, and, lo! on every visage a Black Veil!"
—Mr. Hooper in Hawthorne, "The Minister's Black Veil"

Show me your tits
She thinks I say
When I ask *what's all this?*
Tapping her nib-jabbed essay.

The blue ink's run
As if some rage
Had been shotgunned
Upon the page

Before condensing into tears.
She's wearing latex gloves
Because she blurts she fears
An STD from Jesus whom she loves.

Her classroom oddities
Have grown more violent—
Wild flossing, swatting hair-hived bees—
As she bungles each assignment.

I won't record an F,
But ask her to revise.
She hears *fuck me* as if
All words sexualize

Her nails-scraped-blackboard brain.
Her lungs contort each breath;
Talk stokes a raw migraine.
She'd welcome sleep or death,

But has to pass this class.
I broach a therapist—
She lip-reads *want some ass*
And flees across campus.

Infamous among faculty
Who sympathize but fear her
Fixation on obscenity,
She once received honors:

Our grad-school-bound English major.
Her chemistry's a mystery:
The acumen of a scholar
Combined with helpless deviltry.

Such brilliance. And such horror.

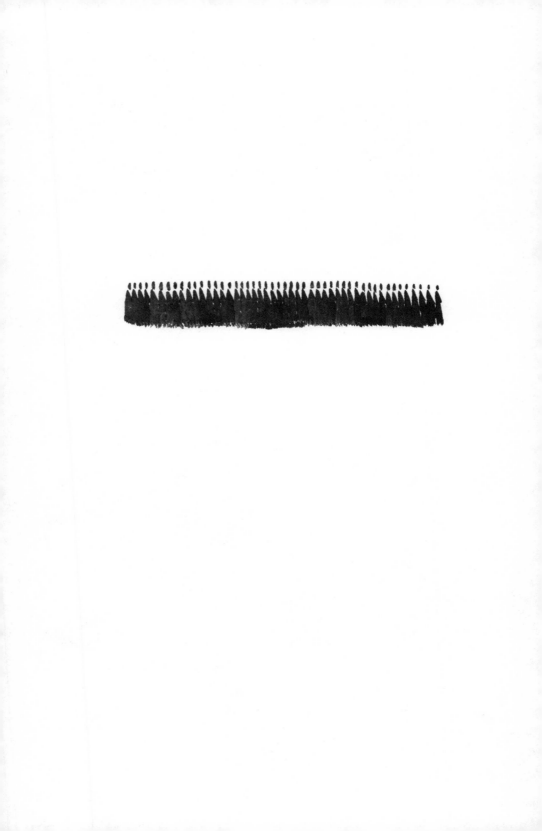

CHERNOBYL NECKLACE

Among "countries that are counterfeits of Death,"
Baudelaire in 1846 could not foresee Belarus
Where throats festooned with red crescent scars
Grin across schoolrooms and orphanage wards.

Even an aesthete like Gérard de Nerval
Who leashed his lobster for a stroll to the opera
Could not divine this couture of the doomed—
Post-op jewelry where butterfly-shaped

Thyroids blackened, then bloomed.

ȚIGANCĂ

photograph from Romania, 1958

Firebombed in his flat—
    the government had banned nomadism—
    her grandfather ashed into unspoken history
    with the family's helpless, communal complicity.

Now this kodachrome—
    her girl-mother aura'd in blueblack hair,
    aflame in the molten silks of her tribe,
    the hammered clamor of scarves and shawls,

Foreseeing the future
    where her grown daughter still protects her
    by never remarking the crow-like visage
    or coppery complexion, never braising

The Christmas rabbit
    with mustard seed and olive brine: such aroma
    suffusing the folk song her father once hummed,
    a lullaby of lament for his Gypsy wife,

O where can she be tonight?

LETTER TO STERN FROM SUCEAVA

J:
    The waitress upon whom I've bestowed
A vulgar sobriquet, Titsecu,
If only to vex my faux-jealous wife
Who asks if I'd flirted enough to learn
Her name (I'd hunkered down to write a poem),
Would prod you to sing some '40s standard
Or apt "Romania, Romania,"
Not because she doesn't know how sorry
Her future in this town will be. She does.
She unbuttons her soiled, unisex smock,
Café Tzara sewn in cursive above
One sentry-stiff breast, just as her girlfriend
Skids the Ducati curbside. And she's off.
I imagine you here among street kids
Who'd trail you, your rabbinical piping,
From train station and dump and sewer nerves
To the only crêpe stall that serves Gypsies.
Almost ninety, you'd boom out brotherhood—
That worn word—as your lice-ridden parade
Revved past pyramids of rat-gray rubble,
The lunar ruins of this post-comm muddle.
The waitress might hear you and, if she knew,
Almost forgive me. *Titsecu*, I tease
As my wife struggles not to unfrown.
Tough Titsecu.
                    Ever yr bad boy,
                        M

SUCEVIȚA MONASTERY

15th C
Bucovina, Romania

Scaffolding's still rigged along wick-burnt walls
Where the homesick monk lay on his back
On the uppermost plank, skull
Propped by his coarse cowl,

A squirrel-hair brush tipped in blue
Dabbing a fold of the Virgin's robe,
                           a blue
The precise shade of roiled sky viewed

Through this ruined roof
Open to swallows, each stone slab
Underfoot
Struck by a whistle of light quickly

Cloud-snuffed, cast back into shadow
Where I remain,
                lost Host,
                         seized

Within Your fierce and faithless gaze.

VORONEȚ BLUE

painted monastery (1487)
Bucovina, Romania

Not the unrepentant blue of the northern
  Romanian summer sky, nor
    The imperishable blue

Of the once-glimpsed & homely
  False water spider orchid,
    Nor . . . I will stop now

Because "*false*" has fastened
  Its meaning with one impatient
    Syllable to language

Riven by romance, like graffito
  Scraped by thumbnail
    Onto the smoke-drabbed

Monastery wall: *Homesick /*
  Wm. Babington / 1826
    Who might have read the dead

Keats before offering himself
  Unto such blasé posterity. But
    "Might have" is less than "*false*"

To any philosopher-by-the-hour
  Or think-tank guru who gauges
    The extent of our millennial

Loneliness. Voroneț blue
  Has survived five centuries
    While no artist has replicated

Its exact, soul-swirled depth
　　Nor analysis fathomed
　　　　Its chemical components.

Sometimes simple facts
　　Seem enough to draw this world
　　　　Into the next epoch where

Our language will remain
　　False, our human, almost
　　　　Helpless approximation

Allowing us to weigh
　　Each semblance of beauty,
　　　　Each version of decay,

God's water spider orchid
　　Not "*imperishable blue*,"
　　　　But close to Voroneț.

LORD COCKROACH

Near-dead roaches seem enraptured in prayer,
Rocking their sleek sheaths, papery coffins,
As they tease out one leg, then another,
Uncoil a copper antenna, summon
Roachy gods.
                    Their dying takes forever,
So they hospice themselves on the bathroom's
Honeycombed tiles, dun husks swaddled in dust,
The young lucent as crinkled cellophane,
The two-inch ancients umber shades darker
In their wooden boats, woolen overcoats,
Wings like shrouds carted across continents—
Who fled the sudden light-flood, fled again
The thunderous, percussive lovemaking
In a time of famine, a time of war.
Their dying takes forever, so I bear
Each body with tender care in crumpled
Tissue, then let fall the brittle faithful
Into still waters quickly flushed.
                              Their gods
Must think they're witnessing ceremony,
One more ritual in a roach-ruled world
To remind myself, my wary lover
Ill with disgust beneath plush bedcovers,
How on six wiry legs
                    Death
                         approaches.

WOODEN BOAT

—after the painting "Bateau" by Carlo
Collection de l'Art Brut, Lausanne

Cloaked in black, intent upon
The monolithic presence ballasting the prow,
Glyph or abstract sculpture, perhaps a crude
Mineral rendering of some deity
Who beckons us across this sea
Into which the stunned green sky
Empties itself endlessly,
My familiar fellow passengers
Withhold speech, barely breathe,
Quailed with reverence, anticipatory . . .

While, upright and loud, I sing, lustful
Pilgrim secure in the knowledge
That whichever god has summoned me
Amid such bowed and dolorous neighbors
Recognizes how foul my soul must be,
Stung by sex, torn by money, minus mercy.
My soul encompasses the century.
I sing like there's no tomorrow.
I yowl because I've been given voice,
And I've never been so goddamned happy.

NOTES

Epigraphs: Emily Dickinson, from a letter to Elizabeth Holland (1883), qtd. in *The Life of Emily Dickinson, Volumes 1–2*, by Richard B. Sewall (Harvard UP, 1994). Nico, from the song "Afraid" on *Desertshore* (1970).

"*Effata*": for Gail Langstroth, eurythmist.

"Beauty in the World": the song of that title appears on *The Sellout* (2010) by Macy Gray, lyrics and melody by Macy Gray, music by Josh Lopez, George Reichart and Kannon Kross, handclaps by Jared Lee Gosselin, Phillip White and Shelton Rivers.

"Punk Prayer": Lingua Ignota, created by the 12th-century German nun Hildegard von Bingen, is the "first entirely artificial language of which any record survives . . . [Bingen] seems to have used Lingua Ignota for some form of mystical communion . . . All that remains of her language is a short passage and a dictionary of a thousand and twelve words listed in hierarchical order, from the most important (*Aigonz*, God) to the least (*Caviz*, cricket)." —Joshua Foer, "Utopian for Beginners," *The New Yorker*, Dec. 24 & 31, 2012.

"American Songbook": jazz singer Susannah McCorkle recorded numerous albums of popular standards and performed at Carnegie Hall and Lincoln Center, as well as at cabarets, such as The Cookery in Greenwich Village. We met at Yaddo in 1983.

"Old Country Recipes": in memory of Kurt Brown (1944–2013).

"Blackbirds": this found poem is taken verbatim from *Bringing It All Back Home* by Ian Clayton (UK: Route Publishing, 2008), qtd. in *A Brief History of Whistling* by John Lucas and Allan Chatburn (UK: Five Leaves, 2013).

"Sixties Sonnet": anthropologist Napoleon A. Chagnon, in a letter to *The New York Times Magazine* (March 3, 2013), writes: "I object to the notion that whether the tribe I studied is called 'Yanomamö' or 'Yanomami' is a matter of preference. It is a matter of linguistics. The final vowel /ö/ in Yanomamö is important; some people don't hear it and therefore cannot pronounce the name that the Yanomamö use for themselves. If the name is rendered 'Yanomami,' people pronounce it 'Yanoma-meee.' This mispronunciation can be traced to members of the Catholic missions in Venezuela and Brazil who came from countries where Romance languages are spoken and had trouble hearing the final vowel /ö/. The rendition of the tribal name as 'Yanomami' gives me an uncomfortable feeling that I am subscribing to and endorsing a 500-year legacy of Spanish, Portuguese and French colonialism among Native Americans in the New World. I hope outsiders will take this into consideration when they adopt a spelling for the tribal name." Okay. Peace.

"The Captain's Tower": the quoted passages are taken from the obituary of Eli Wilentz ("Eli Wilentz, Whose Bookstore Lured the 'Beats,' Is Dead at 76"), *The New York Times*, June 26, 1995. The misheard song lyric is, of course, from "Tiny Dancer" (1971), written by Elton John and Bernie Taupin, which reads, "Hold me closer tiny dancer."

"Mihaela Barefoot": the last line owes a debt to "Where does such tenderness come from?" by Marina Tsvetaeva, written for Osip Mandelstam in 1916, version by Ilya Kaminsky and Jean Valentine in *Dark Elderberry Branch: Poems of Marina Tsvetaeva* (Alice James Books, 2012).

"The Scavengers": this found poem, scavenged then altered slightly, shapes portions of "Of Compost, Molecules and Insects, Art Is Born" by Natalie Angier, *The New York Times*, May 3, 2010. Several phrases are of my own making.

"Quoting Rumi": in Persian, *zakar* means "penis," a word found often in Rumi's poems. In "The Hermeneutics of Eroticism in the Poetry of Rumi" in *Comparative Studies of South Asia, Africa and the Middle East*, Vol. 25, No. 3 (2005), Mahdi Tourage suggests that Rumi's use of "bawdy passages" and habit of "incorporating vulgar words . . . may be viewed as a form of resistance against literary decorum and the conventions of mystical poetry." *Change of Habit* (1969) starred Elvis

Presley as Dr. John Carpenter and Mary Tyler Moore as undercover novitiate Sister Michelle Gallagher.

"Jade Garden": the quoted passage is from "To the Reader" by Charles Baudelaire, trans. Stanley Kunitz in *The Poems of Stanley Kunitz 1928–1978* (Atlantic Monthly Press, 1979).

"Chernobyl Necklace": the quoted passage, altered slightly, is from "Anywhere Out of the World" by Charles Baudelaire in *Paris Spleen*, trans. Louise Varèse (New Directions, 1970).

"Letter to Stern from Suceava": the word "unfrown" is stolen from Theodore Roethke. The name of the waitress should be pronounced with affection.

"Voroneţ Blue": "Perhaps the most famous and stunning of the painted monasteries is Voroneţ *(Vo ro nets)*, founded in 1487 by Stephen the Great to celebrate a victory over the Turks. Widely known throughout Europe as 'the Sistine Chapel of the East' due to its interior and exterior wall paintings, this monastery offers an abundance of frescoes featuring an intense shade of blue commonly known as 'Voroneţ blue.' The composition of the paint continues to remain a mystery even now, more than 500 years after the church was built." —www.romaniatourism. com/painted-monasteries.html. I first visited the painted monasteries of Bucovina, Romania, in 1998, and have returned to them several times since.

"Wooden Boat": triggered by "Bateau" by outsider artist Carlo (1916–1974), 35 x 50 cm, gouache, in Collection de l'Art Brut, Lausanne, Switzerland. I viewed the painting in 2004.

ACKNOWLEDGMENTS

Warm thanks for their generous support to the editors and staffs of the journals and anthologies in which these poems, sometimes in earlier versions, appeared:

America: "Old Country Recipes";
The American Poetry Review: "The Book of Names," "Dominoes," "Lord Cockroach," "Marvel," "Mihaela Barefoot," "The New Gods," "Old School," "Poem, Slow to Come, on the Death of Logan," "Punk Prayer," "Sixties Sonnet," "Tic Tac Toe";
Arts & Letters: "American Songbook," "The Beatles";
Cardinal Points: "Chernobyl Necklace," "Eve's Daughter";
5 A.M.: "Old Records," "Sick Student";
Gargoyle: "Horse," "Last Day on Ios," "Quoting Rumi," "Voroneṭ Blue";
The Georgia Review: "Madrigal";
The Gettysburg Review: "*Effata*," "Morning Run";
Poetry International: "Beauty in the World," "Letter to Stern from Suceava";
Review Revue: "The Captain's Tower";
Southern Humanities Review: "Erotic Amphora";
Southern Indiana Review: "Țigancă," "Wooden Boat";
Spillway: "Dog Ears," "Jade Garden," "Pottery Sale," "Sucevița Monastery."

Several poems were reprinted in *Alecart* (Romania), *B O D Y* (Czech Republic), *Great River Review*, *Hearing Voices* (UK), *Sleipnir*, *This Broken Shore*, *Vox Populi* and, in translation by Mihaela Moscaliuc, *Convorbiri Literare* and *Poezia* (Romania).

"Dominoes" was reprinted in *Poetry Calendar 2013*, ed. Shafiq Naz (Bertem, Belgium: Alhambra, 2012).

"*Effata*" was reprinted in *Heartland: A Portfolio of Poems and Prints*, ed. Robert Hedin (Anderson Center for Interdisciplinary Studies, 2015).

"Madrigal" was reprinted in *Poems & Their Making*, ed. Philip Brady (Etruscan Press, 2015).

"Old Country Recipes" was reprinted in *Eating Our Words: Poets Share Their Favorite Recipes*, ed. Kurt Brown (Tupelo Press, 2016).

"Punk Prayer" was reprinted in *Poetry in the Blood*, ed. Tony Roberts (Nottingham, UK: Shoestring Press, 2014).

"Sixties Sonnet" was reprinted in *Far Out: Poems of the Sixties*, eds. Wendy Barker and David M. Parsons (Wings Press, 2016).

Excerpt from "Desolation Row" by Bob Dylan: Copyright © 1965 by Warner Bros. Inc.; renewed 1993 by Special Rider Music. All rights reserved. International copyright secured. Reprinted by permission.

I remain grateful to the New Jersey State Council on the Arts for a 2012 Individual Artist Fellowship, and to Monmouth University for Grant-in-Aid for Creativity Awards in 2012 and 2014 which allowed me to spend time in Romania and which supported a residency fellowship at the Virginia Center for the Creative Arts, respectively. Thanks also to the VCCA for the time and space in which to complete this book, and to Monmouth University, again, for a sabbatical leave during 2014–15.

Support of a less tangible but still substantial kind during the writing of this manuscript was provided by friends, including Kimiko Hahn, Robert Hedin, William Heyen, John Hoppenthaler, Ilya Kaminsky, Maxine Kumin (1925–2014), John Lucas, Shara McCallum, Laura McCullough, Ron Mitchell, Alicia Ostriker, Harold Schechter, Elizabeth Spires, David St. John, Gerald Stern, Susan Terris, Liliana Ursu and, especially, Judith Vollmer, as well as by my daughter, Kiernan, terrestrial joyrider, and my wife, Mihaela Moscaliuc, without whom. . . .

In memory of Nina Cassian (1924–2014) and Louis Simpson (1923–2012).

ABOUT THE AUTHOR

Michael Waters teaches at Monmouth University and in the Drew University MFA Program in Poetry and Poetry in Translation. His books include *Gospel Night* (2011), *Darling Vulgarity* (2006—finalist for the *Los Angeles Times* Book Prize), and *Parthenopi: New and Selected Poems* (2001—finalist for the Paterson Poetry Prize). He is co-editor of *Contemporary American Poetry* (2006) and *Perfect in Their Art: Poems on Boxing from Homer to Ali* (2003). The recipient of five Pushcart Prizes and fellowships from the National Endowment for the Arts, the Fulbright Foundation, the Ledig-Rowohlt Foundation, and the New Jersey State Council on the Arts, he lives in Ocean, NJ.

BOA EDITIONS, LTD.
AMERICAN POETS CONTINUUM SERIES

COLOPHON

BOA Editions, Ltd., a not-for-profit publisher of poetry and other literary works, fosters readership and appreciation of contemporary literature. By identifying, cultivating, and publishing both new and established poets and selecting authors of unique literary talent, BOA brings high-quality literature to the public. Support for this effort comes from the sale of its publications, grant funding, and private donations.

The publication of this book is made possible, in part, by the special support of the following individuals:

Anonymous x 3
Anonymous, *in memory of A. Poulin, Jr.*
Nin Andrews
Angela Bonazinga & Catherine Lewis
Nickole Brown & Jessica Jacobs
Bernadette Catalana
Christopher & DeAnna Cebula
Gwen & Gary Conners
Anne C. Coon & Craig J. Zicari
Gouvernet Arts Fund
Michael Hall, *in memory of Lorna Hall*
Grant Holcomb
Christopher Kennedy & Mi Ditmar
X. J. & Dorothy M. Kennedy
Keetje Kuipers & Sarah Fritsch, *in memory of JoAnn Wood Graham*
Jack & Gail Langerak
Daniel M. Meyers, *in honor of James Shepard Skiff*
Boo Poulin
Deborah Ronnen & Sherman Levey
Steven O. Russell & Phyllis Rifkin-Russell
Sue S. Stewart, *in memory of Stephen L. Raymond*
Lynda & George Waldrep
Michael & Patricia Wilder